BASS

C

Traditional Fiddling in the String Orchestra

Andrew H. Dabczynski
&
Bob Phillips

Cover design: Ruth McKinney & Leslie Ann Levine
Cover photos: Fiddle/Marty Lebenson
        Autumn Scene/Corel Corporation

Interior production: Greg Plumblee
Illustrations: Pamela E. Phillips

2

Dr. Andrew H. Dabczynski

Dr. Andrew H. Dabczynski is Supervisor of Fine Arts Education in the Waterford School District in Michigan, and serves as a guest conductor throughout North America. He received a B.M. from the Eastman School of Music, an M.A. from the University of Connecticut and a Ph.D. in Music Education from the University of Michigan where he wrote his doctoral dissertation on how fiddle music is taught and learned today. He has taught at Concordia College in New York, Olivet College in Michigan, the University of Connecticut, the American String Workshop, the International String Workshop, the Institute for String Teaching and the Mamaroneck Public Schools in New York.

Dr. Dabczynski is a string consultant and editor for Boosey and Hawkes. He studied with members of the Juilliard, Amadeus, Fine Arts, Eastman and New England string quartets, and was the violist with the Colden String Quartet at Western Michigan University. He performs today on fiddle as a member of the Irish group Modesty Forbids, and presents workshops on the use of traditional music in orchestra and string classes.

Bob Phillips

Bob Phillips is orchestra director for the Saline Area Schools in Saline, Michigan. He is founder and artistic director of the high school folk fiddling ensemble, Fiddlers Philharmonic. He received his B.M. and M.M. from the University of Michigan, where he studied with double bassist Lawrence Hurst.

Mr. Phillips has presented clinics throughout the United States, including the International String Workshop, the National String Workshop, the American String Workshop, the Mid-West International Band and Orchestra Clinic, and the International Society of Bassists convention. He has served as conductor for the All-State Orchestra at Interlochen, the Michigan Honors Orchestra, the Blue Lake Fine Arts Camp, the Jackson Youth Symphony and the Oakland Youth Orchestra. In 1993 he was the Michigan School Band and Orchestra Association Orchestra Teacher of the Year, and in 1996 was named the American String Teachers Association Michigan Teacher of the Year.

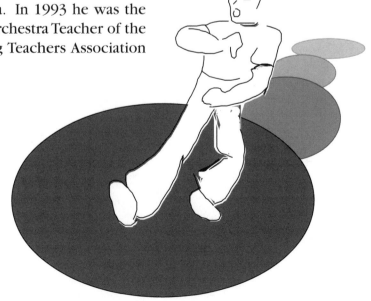

Table of Contents

Introduction

Fiddlers Philharmonic has developed out of a love for music in all its many styles and forms. Folk music in general and fiddling in particular are vital parts of our rich cultural heritage which provide access for the string player to a whole world of music making. We feel fiddle music offers a vast pedagogical and motivational resource that can only enhance the musical development of any string player.

With these things in mind, we felt the need to organize a collection of fiddling materials for the benefit of the entire string program, not just the violin section. Designed to complement the school string curriculum, these books and sound recordings can also be used by private teachers in the studio. A series of contrasting traditional fiddle tunes is offered in a carefully constructed pedagogical order. First, each tune is presented in the best key for solo playing. An arrangement follows, in the most appropriate common key for simultaneous performance by all instruments. In the individual books, this arrangement includes the melody, a variation or "break," a "back-up" accompaniment part and a bass line. Chord symbols are also presented so that guitars, autoharps, pianos or other instruments can join the group. Students may play the individual line that best fits their ability level, and the arrangements are constructed so that any combination of instruments and parts will sound good. The flexible nature of the arrangements allows advanced students to play a challenging "break" or improvised solo even while a beginner plays a simple, open-string, "back-up" harmony part. In this way, each player is participating to the fullest and everyone is making a genuine contribution to the music. This is the authentic essence of folk music, and promises to provide enjoyment and success for students of any skill level or age.

For centuries, fiddle tunes have been passed through the generations "by ear," so a sound recording has been produced to provide students with an opportunity to learn the tunes in the traditional manner. By learning from and playing along with the recording, students can develop critical ear-training and improvisation skills. Meanwhile, they gain an appreciation for the stylistic differences that define various fiddling traditions. We recommend that students and teachers use the books and tapes in combination, as each complements the other.

Most importantly, we urge you to rosin up the bow, dive in, and have fun! Keep those toes tapping and remember, dancing in the aisles is allowed!

Bob and Andy

4

Although its origins are difficult to determine, this tune is often played and has been adapted to many different styles. One thing for sure is that *Cripple Creek* is an old tune named after a stream located someplace between Georgia and Oregon! Adding a flatted seventh in a solo with many fast-moving notes gives the tune a hard-driving bluegrass sound.

Cripple Creek
SOLO KEY

Tune/Break/Back-Up
Tracks 2, 3

GROUP KEY

For over three hundred years, fishing has been a major occupation in Newfoundland, Canada's easternmost province. *I'se the B'y* is an old Newfoundland seafaring song and makes a great fiddling jig. Try to alternate singing and playing the melody for added interest.

I'se the B'y
SOLO KEY

I'se the b'y that builds the boat,
I'se the b'y that sails her.
I'se the b'y that catches the fish,
And brings 'em home to Liza.*
    *or Lizer

I took Liza to the dance;
Faith but she could travel.
Ev'ry step that Liza took,
Covered an acre of gravel.

Salt and rinds to cover your flake,
Cake and tea for supper.
Codfish in the spring of the year,
Fried in maggoty butter.

Susan White, she's out of sight,
Her petticoat wants a border,
Old Sam Oliver in the dark,
He kissed her in the corner.

Tune/Break/Back-Up

GROUP KEY

Perhaps one of the simplest yet most satisfying hoe-downs, for the beginner or the expert fiddler, is *Bile 'em Cabbage Down*. The four-note melody can be combined with creative improvisation to produce increasingly complicated variations. Here's a tune for every fiddler.

Bile 'em Cabbage Down

SOLO KEY

Chorus:
Bile 'em cabbage down, down,
Bake 'em biskets brown, brown.
Only tune I ever did learn was,
Bile 'em cabbage down.

Verse:
June bug he has wings of gold,
The firefly wings of flame.
The bedbug's got no wings at all,
But gets there just the same.

Love it is a killing fit,
When beauty hits a blossom,
And if you want your finger bit,
Just poke it at a possum.

Raccoon and the possum,
Rackin' cross the prairie,
Raccoon asks the possum,
Did she want to marry?

Possum is a cunnin' thing,
He travels in the dark,
And never thinks to curl his tail,
Till he hears old Rover bark.

Tune/Break/Back-Up Tracks 6, 7

GROUP KEY

8

Si Bheag Si Mhor is a beautiful old Irish air, usually played simply and leisurely, and occasionally played as a waltz. The tune is attributed to the blind harpist and singer Turlough Carolan (1670–1738), who is considered by many to be one of Ireland's most important composers. The Gaelic title of this tune literally means "So Big, So Little," and seems to have some relationship to legends about the hills that were home to mythical fairies. The melody invites ornamentation, simple harmonies and accompanying drones.

Si Bheag Si Mhor
SOLO KEY

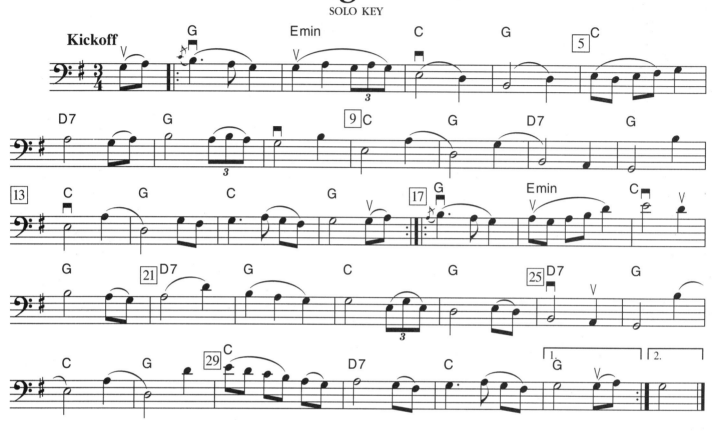

Tune/Harmony/Back-Up

Tracks 8, 9

GROUP KEY

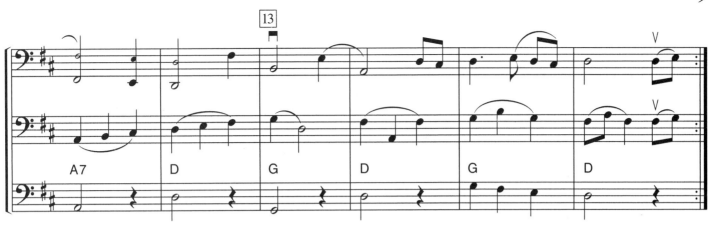

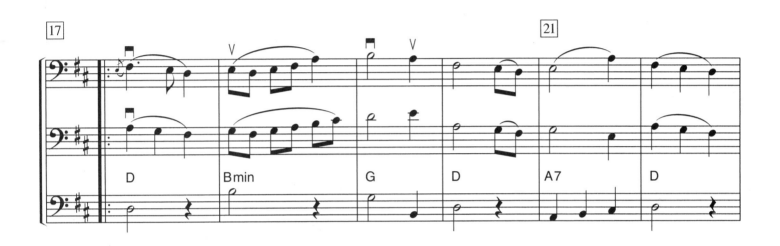

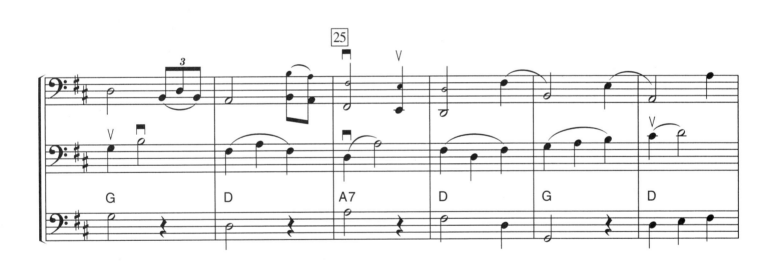

9

Road to Boston has an obvious relationship to New England and is heard commonly as a contra dance reel in that region. Variations of the tune and alternate titles (such as *On the Road*, *Boston March* and *Road to London*) suggest that it probably originated in Great Britain, perhaps dating from the early eighteenth century. Try playing the reel with a bounce and a lift for a real contra dance feel.

Road to Boston

SOLO KEY

Tune/Break/Back-Up

Tracks 10, 11

GROUP KEY

Old Joe Clark is an old, well-known American folk song with more silly verses than can be counted. A few sets of words are offered here—try to come up with some of your own! The melody is in Mixolydian mode, which means it has a lowered seventh scale step. By adding a "shuffle" and lots of rhythmic accents, it becomes an exciting, hard-driving fiddle tune.

Old Joe Clark
SOLO KEY

Verse:

Old Joe Clark he had a house, fifteen stories high.
Ev'ry story in that house was filled with chicken pie.

I went down to Old Joe's house, he was eating supper.
Stubbed my toe on a table leg, and rammed my nose in the butter.

Old Joe Clark he had a wife, and she was eight feet tall,
She slept with her head on the kitchen stove, and her feet stuck in the hall.

Had a banjo made o' gold, strings were made of twine,
Only tune that I could play, "Wish That Gal Were Mine."

Chorus:

Round an' round Old Joe Clark, Round an' round we're gone,
Round an' round Old Joe Clark and goodbye, Lucy Long.

Tune/Break/Back-Up

GROUP KEY

14

Dorian mode is frequently used in Irish fiddle tunes, such as *Swallowtail Jig*. Playing drones and open strings along with the tune, and emphasizing the strong beat in the accompaniment enhance the dark sound of the mode. *Swallowtail Jig* followed by *Kesh Jig* makes a great medley with effective contrasts.

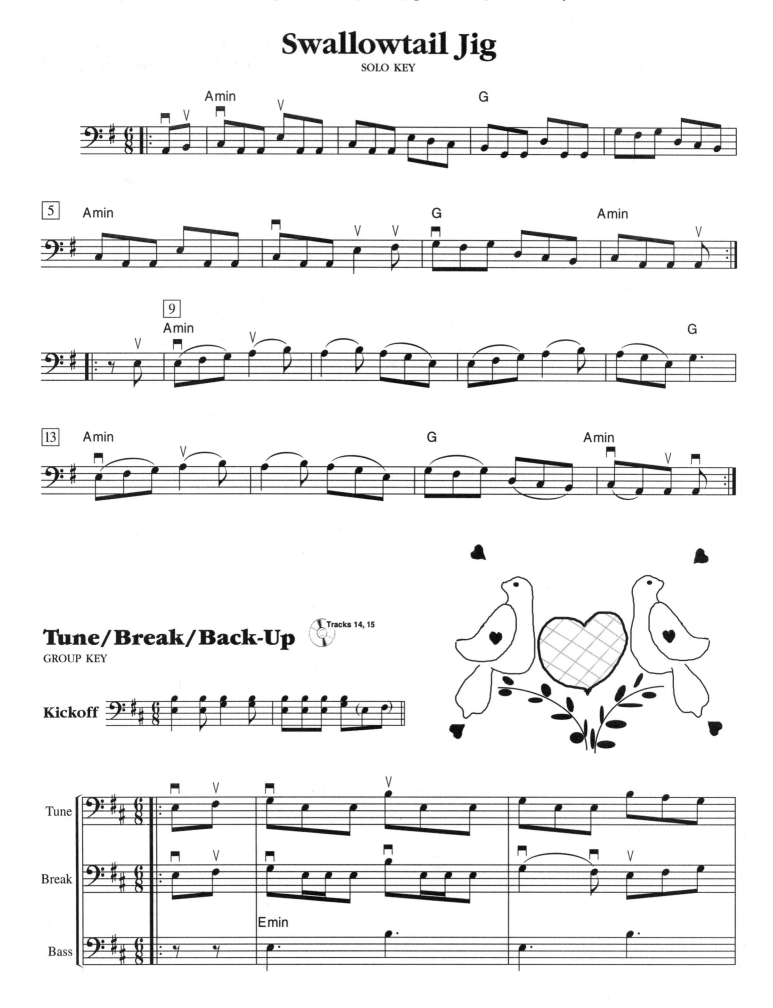

Ash Grove represents the extensive folk music tradition of Wales. It is frequently sung with lyrics that illustrate its flowing melody. Along with the fiddle, the familiar melody is often played by the recorder, tin whistle, piano or guitar. A versatile air, *Ash Grove* is sometimes given a stronger beat and played as a waltz.

Ash Grove
SOLO KEY

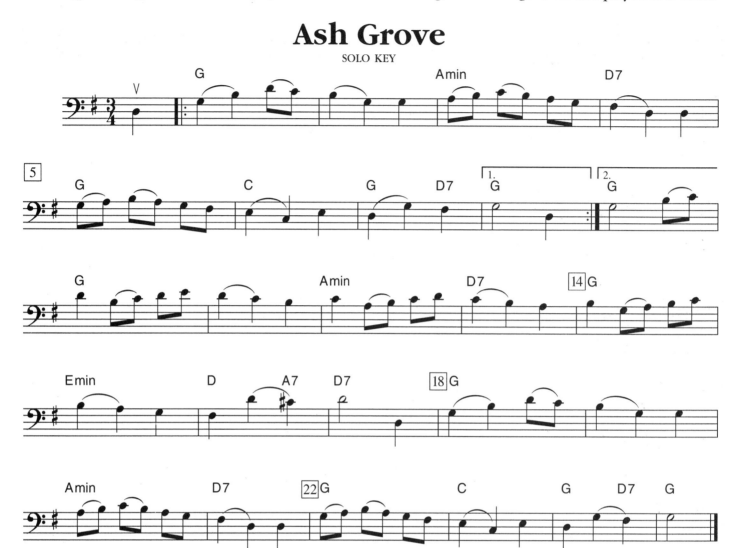

The ash grove how graceful, How plainly 'tis speaking,
The harp through it playing has language for me;
Whenever the light through its branches is breaking,
A host of kind faces is gazing on me.
The friends of my childhood again are before me,
Each step wakes a mem'ry as freely I roam;
With whispers laden, its leaves rustle o'er me;
The ash grove, the ash grove alone is my home.

*On mahlos ilween on gint, veh drigipen devig.
Evehoith us gwiahr ok ahgloo'ith uh wlad;
Ok eethoeen eneth uh anoid uneenig,
Uh henol eer hones oith irees i thod,
Eith caryod you gwailed un lan uh feer lenken,
Ond codire us gwiahr un ovahr ok airch,
Ee saitheer bach genen, ond gweer othi linin,
lairged un oorgam ee vunwee i vairch.

*Phonetic Welsh text from *Folk Songs of England, Ireland,
Scotland and Wales* by William Cole © 1961 Doubleday Books.
Reprinted here by kind permission of William Cole and Doubleday.

Tune/Break/Back-Up
 Tracks 16, 17

GROUP KEY

Flowers of Edinburgh is an old Scottish tune that can be traced back at least to 1750. In one early collection of fiddle tunes, the "flowers" of Edinburgh are said to have been the judges and lawyers of the town. The rhythmic "Scottish Snap" in this version gives it a characteristic flair.

Flowers of Edinburgh
SOLO KEY

Tune/Break/Back-Up
Tracks 18, 19

GROUP KEY

La Valse des Jeunes Filles, or *Waltz of the Little Girls* is a French tune that has started to become part of the New England and French-Canadian fiddling repertoires. This pleasant waltz sounds particularly good with a light, uncomplicated accompaniment that reflects the gentle mood of the title.

La Valse des Jeunes Filles
SOLO KEY

Tune/Break/Back-Up
Tracks 20, 21

GROUP KEY

Kickoff

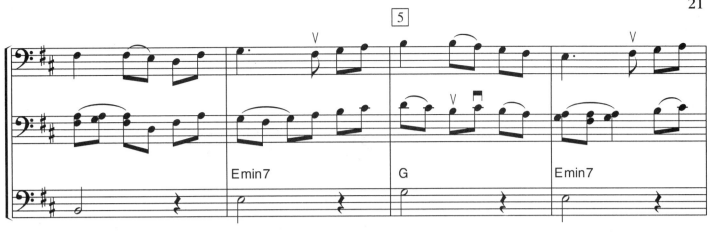

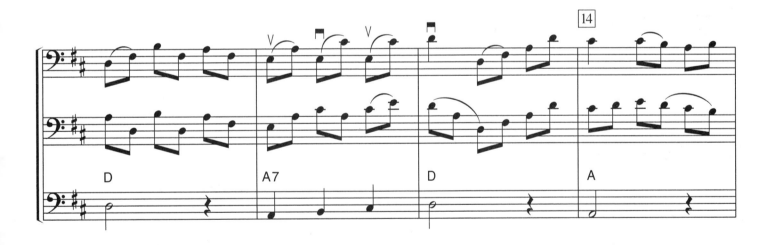

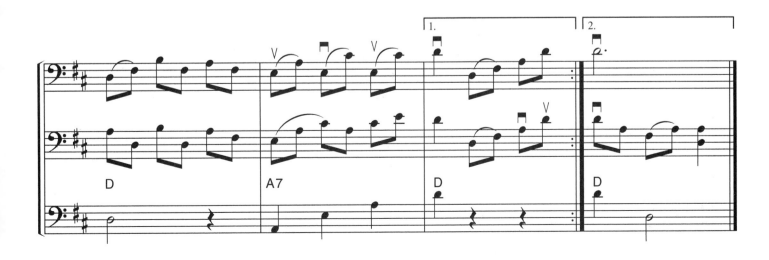

Along with the massive nineteenth-century Irish immigration to the United States came the traditional music of the Irish countryside. The music thrived in North America, particularly in the large urban concentrations of Irish immigrants. The Irish style has had a great impact on the folk music and dances of the United States and Canada. *Kesh Jig* is a prime example of an Irish jig that has become a standard among fiddlers in the "New World." It invites the addition of ornamentation and other variations.

Kesh Jig
SOLO KEY

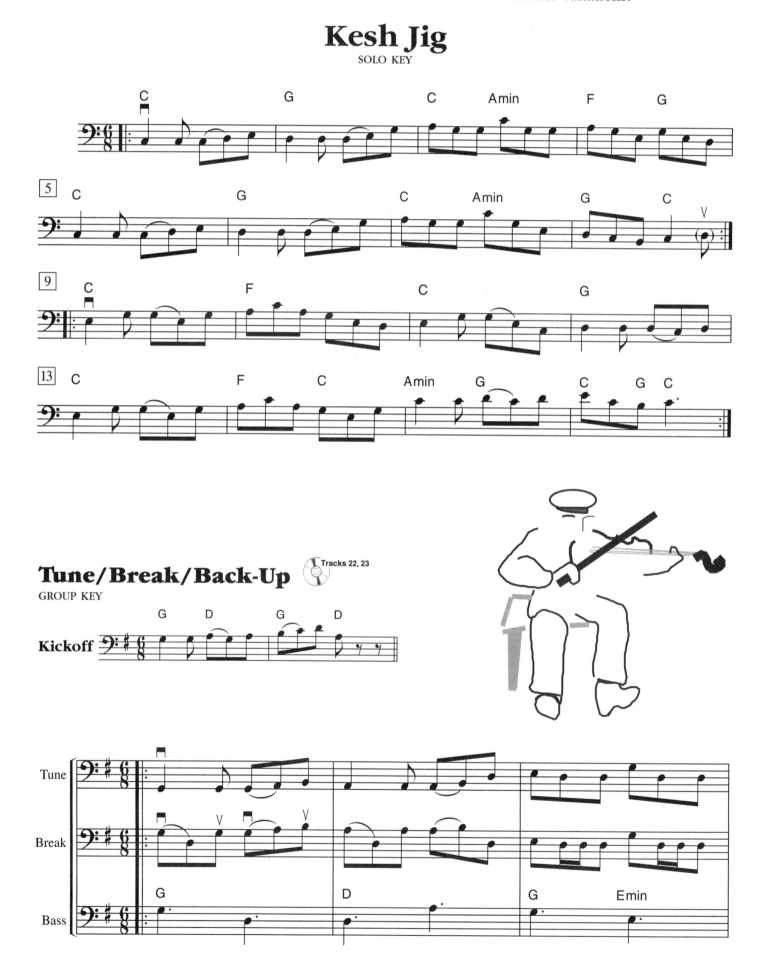

Tune/Break/Back-Up Tracks 22, 23
GROUP KEY

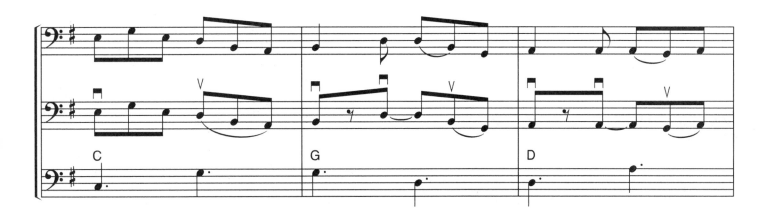

24

Westphalia Waltz is a comfortable, relaxing tune. One of the most common fiddle waltzes, its simple, uncomplicated melody adapts well to a variety of styles. *Westphalia Waltz* is often played by New England, bluegrass, Old-Timey, and even French-Canadian fiddlers.

Westphalia Waltz
SOLO KEY

Tune/Break/Back-Up

GROUP KEY

26

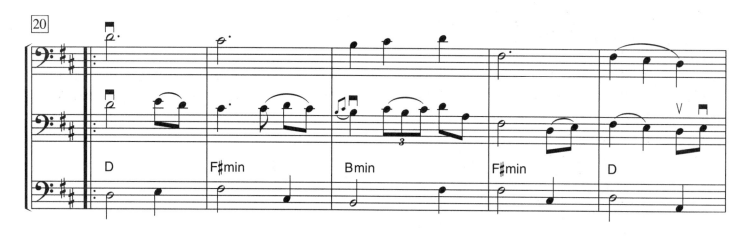

The use of fiddles in Scandinavian folk music is a long and established tradition. Common in Swedish fiddling is the use of multiple fiddle parts, creating a rich and sometimes complex harmony. A *gånglåt*, or walking tune, is one of the many functional musical forms common in Swedish fiddle music. The gånglåt, often with roots in one community (such as Mockfjärd), is played by musicians as they parade from village to village, gathering fiddlers as they go. You'll know the tempo of this tune is just right if you can comfortably walk along while playing it.

Gånglåt Från Mockfjärd

SOLO KEY

Tune/Harmony/Back-Up

 Tracks 26, 27

GROUP KEY

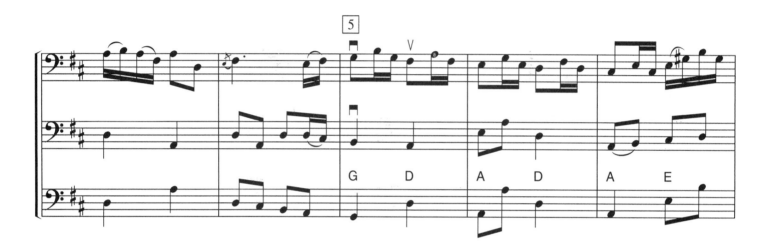

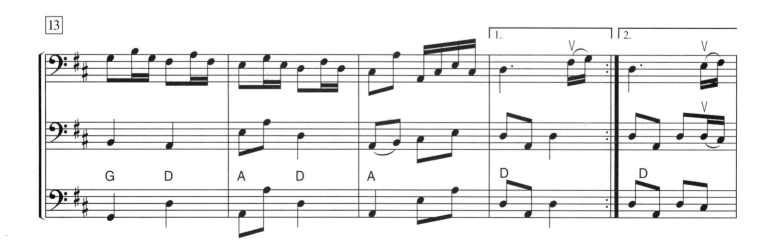

St. Anne's Reel is an example of the New England fiddling style found throughout the Northeastern United States. New England fiddling has its roots in the British Isles and often functions as music for the contra dances that are so popular in the New England/Mid-Atlantic region. The solid beat and pleasing melody make *St. Anne's Reel* a favorite contra dance tune.

St. Anne's Reel
SOLO KEY

Tune/Break/Back-Up
 Tracks 28, 29

GROUP KEY

19 **Transition**

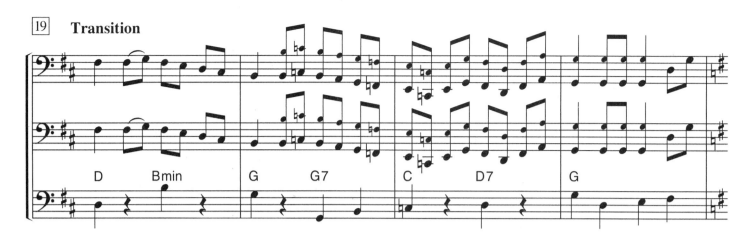

23

27

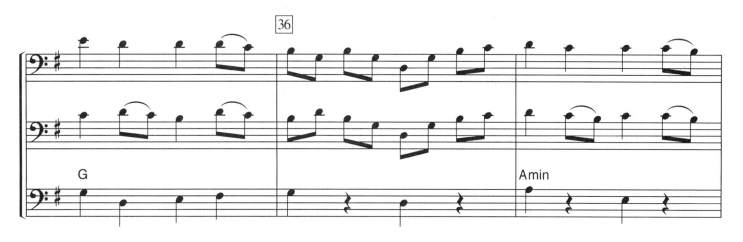

G

Amin

D

G

G

41 **Transition**

G

E

E7

A

A7

D.S. al CODA

CODA ✪
Tag

D

D

A

D

34

Hornpipes are widely played by fifers and concertina players, as well as fiddlers. *Rickett's Hornpipe* is just such a versatile tune. Supposedly, the title refers to an American circus man who was active in the 1790s. The end of the arrangement here, with the parts in parallel harmony, gives this version of *Rickett's Hornpipe* a bit of a Western Swing sound.

Rickett's Hornpipe

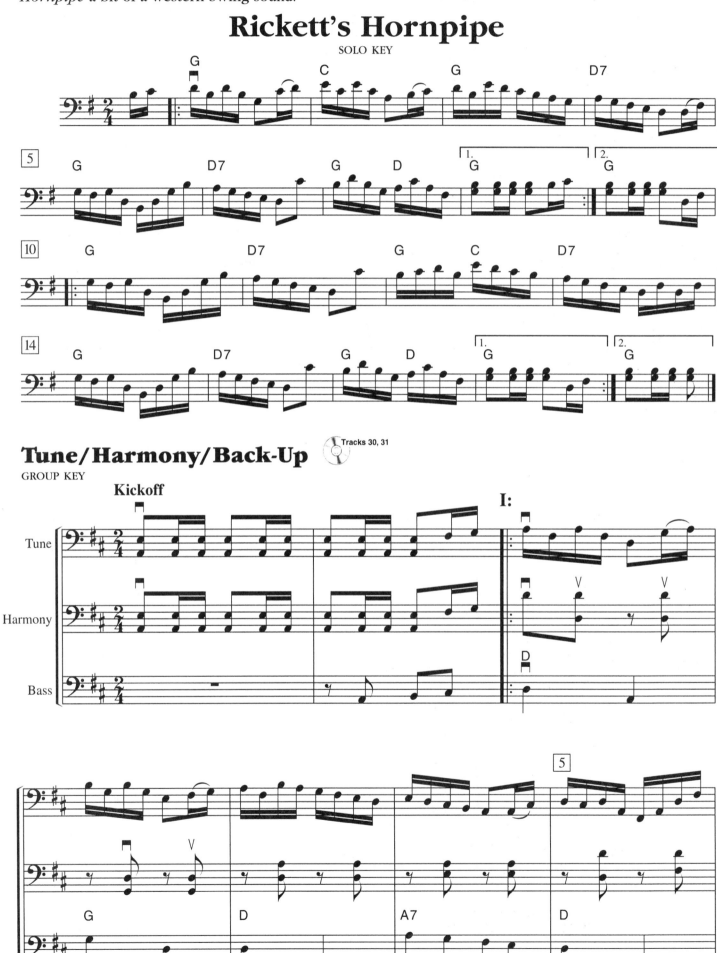

Tune/Harmony/Back-Up

Tracks 30, 31

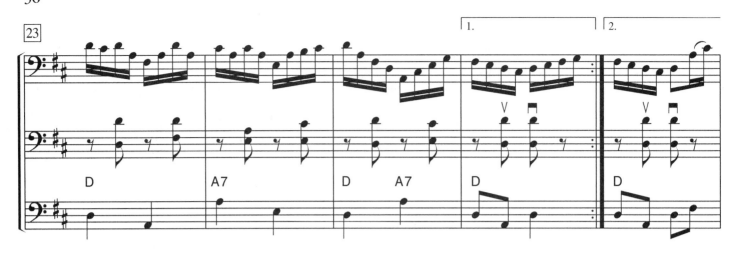

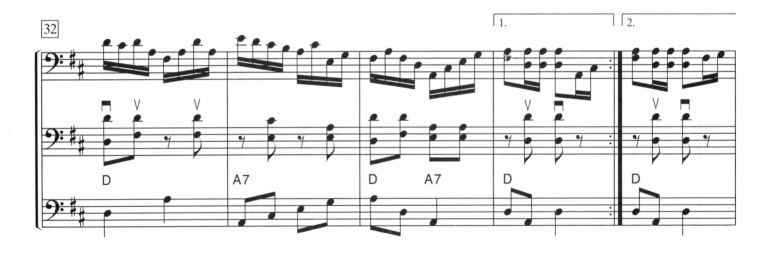

III: Swing

38

In the early decades of the twentieth century, jazz sounds began to influence many fiddlers, particularly in Texas and the Southwest. New country rag tunes entered the repertoire, with emphasis on flashy, creative variations and a swing feel in both the melody and back-up parts. This version of *Swinging Fiddles* captures the essence of Western Swing-style fiddling, with jazzy rhythms and chromatic alterations.

Swinging Fiddles
SOLO KEY

Tune/Break/Back-Up

Tracks 32, 33

GROUP KEY

Glossary

Air: Another word for *air* is tune. An air can be a song with instrumental accompaniment or for several voices. In traditional folk music, an air is often considered an instrumental piece whose melodic style is similar to that of a solo song.

Back-Up: In traditional fiddling, a *back-up* part is an accompanying musical line, rather than the main melody. It may be primarily rhythmic or harmonic, or a combination of both. A back-up part often includes counterpoint.

Bluegrass: In the 1940s, a Kentucky musician named Bill Monroe formed a band which developed its own distinctive sound. By mixing elements of Appalachian mountain music with blues, Irish, jazz, swing and other musical styles, the group soon had a special flavor and an intense, hard-driving feel that was unmistakable. It became known as *bluegrass,* after the name of the band, Bill Monroe and the Bluegrass Boys.

Break: A *break* is a solo variation, usually improvised, based on the basic melodic, harmonic and rhythmic ideas of a tune.

Celtic: *Celtic* refers to the language, customs, beliefs, history, etc., of the Celts, the European people now represented by the Irish, Scottish and Welsh.

Concertina: A version of the accordion, the *concertina* was invented in England by a man named Wheatsone in 1829. It has a hexagonal shape and a series of buttons on each side which can play a full chromatic scale. It produces the same note whether the bellows are pressed or drawn.

Contra Dance: Probably taking its name from the English "country dance," a contra dance is a folk dance that first reached great popularity in the late 18th century, and remains a very popular dance form particularly in the Northeastern United States and Eastern Canada. It is danced with two or more couples facing each other who execute a great variety of steps and motions.

Drone: A *drone* is a long, usually low, held note or notes which frequently accompany a melody. It has the effect of the held notes on a bagpipe.

French-Canadian Style Fiddling: A unique style of fiddling has developed in French Canada, principally in the province of Quebec, as a result of the combining of French and British fiddling traditions. Solo fiddling, often accompanied by the fiddler's own feet clogging a strong rhythm, is often associated with this style.

Gaelic: The traditional, ancient language of Ireland (and any of the languages developed from it) is called *Gaelic.*

Gånglåt: A *gånglåt,* or "walking tune," is a Swedish musical form that is meant to accompany that activity, often in parade-like fashion (pronounced gong'-lot).

Hoe-down: *Hoe-down* is a term generally interchangeable with "square dance."

Hornpipe: A *hornpipe* is a type of dance, as well as the tune for that dance, in 4/4 time. It seems to have originated in the British Isles and is often associated with seafaring. Hornpipes are sometimes played with a lilt, but are often performed like reels.

Jig: A *jig* is a type of dance, as well as the tune for that dance, commonly in 6/8 time. A jig is strongly associated with Irish traditions, and many jigs have Irish roots. A *slip jig* is a dance/tune in 9/8 time.

Kickoff: The rhythmic introduction to a fiddle tune, usually a measure or two in length, that sets its tempo and key, is called a *kickoff.*

Lick: A *lick* is a musician's term for a distinctive rhythmic or melodic idea, perhaps an ornamentation, used in improvisation.

Medley: A series of tunes played in succession is called a *medley.* Occasionally, the tunes in a medley are connected by a few measures of introduction or modulation.

Mixolydian: The *mixolydian* mode or scale is like a major scale, except the seventh note is lowered by a half step (half steps lie between the third and fourth, and sixth and seventh scale degrees). Playing the white notes on a piano from G to G creates a mixolydian scale.

Mode: In general, a melodic *mode* is a series of tones as they are arranged in a scale. A large number of modes exist for any given beginning tone (or tonic), depending on the manner in which half- and whole-step intervals are organized. The ancient Greek modes and medieval church modes are well-known examples of these scale patterns.

New England Style Fiddling: Common on the east coast of the United states from Maine to Pennsylvania, *New England style fiddling* has strong British and Irish roots. Because it often is played for contra dances and square dances, the style has a strong beat and lots of minimally ornamented melodies. New England fiddle tunes usually have a solid, 32-bar phrase structure (two repeated 8-bar phrases resulting in an AABB form).

Old-Timey: The term "Old-Time" fiddling can carry lots of meanings and implies many of the features of traditional fiddling in general, such as playing by ear, improvising, using 'nonclassical' playing positions, and playing the repertoire of tunes handed down informally through the generations. *Old-Timey* fiddling is a term frequently reserved for the sound common to the Appalachian mountains and the American Southeast which incorporates these characteristics, among others.

Reel: A *reel* is a dance, as well as the tune for that dance, in 4/4 time or 2/4 time, and has Celtic origins. A reel dance implies that the dancers face each other in parallel lines. Reel tunes are often played to accompany square dances and other types of dances as well.

Scandinavian-Style Fiddling: Fiddle playing has been a strong feature in Scandinavian folk music and social life for centuries. *Scandinavian-style fiddling* is very functional, and commonly accompanies dancing. Rich harmony and drones which emulate the Norwegian Hardanger fiddles are characteristic of this music.

Scottish Snap: A distinctive syncopated rhythm (written as a sixteenth note followed by a dotted eighth note), the *Scottish Snap* is a characteristic of Scottish traditional music. This feature can also be found in the music of other areas in the British Isles.

Shanty: One kind of work song sung by sailors, associated with the days of sailing ships, is called a *shanty.* Shanties usually have a form consisting of many solo verses and a chorus.

Shuffle: A *shuffle* is a repetitive, rhythmic bowing pattern. Perhaps the simplest and most common shuffle is frequently referred to as a Nashville shuffle, consisting of an eighth note followed by two sixteenths.

Swing: *Swing* is the characteristic sound and feel of jazz, particularly of the jazz associated with the period beginning in the 1930s. Ingredients common to a swing feel are syncopation and the playing of even notes with an almost triplet feel. Certain melodic devices (especially chromatic accidentals), complex shuffle patterns and harmonics are also associated with swing.

Tag: A one- or two-bar ending that frequently signals the completion of a fiddle tune or a set of tunes is often called a *tag.*

Waltz: A *waltz* refers to a common dance and its accompanying music, always in 3/4 time. A waltz can be slow or fast, depending on the feel of the tune.

Western Swing-Style Fiddling: *Western Swing-style fiddling* finds its origins in a combination of Southern, Louisiana jazz and cowboy traditions mixed with big-band era swing sounds. Associated with the southwestern region of the United States, this style enjoys a driving swing beat. A particular kind of Western fiddling characterized by complex melodic improvisation, this style is typical of Texas fiddle contests.